COLLINS

KINGS & QUEENS

OF BRITAIN

Written by
Mary Douglas

Illustrated by
Graham Humphreys

Note to parents and teachers

This fascinating introduction to British history aims to give young readers a picture of the men and women who have reigned in Britain from Saxon times to the 1990s, and to draw the reader's attention to some of the major events that happened during the monarchs' reigns.

Some of the dates given for events that occurred in the reigns of the early monarchs may not agree with those in other books. This is because dependable records were not kept in early times. The publishers have verified all the dates given in this book in two independent sources.

The dates shown for each monarch are the years during which they reigned.

CONTENTS

INTRODUCTION

This is a book about the men, women and, in some cases, children who have sat on the British thrones.

Centuries ago, England, Scotland and Wales were ruled by their own princes, kings and queens. By the end of the thirteenth century, Wales and England had come to be ruled over by the same monarch.

Queen Elizabeth I had no children to inherit the throne. When she died in 1603, it passed to James I, the son of her cousin Mary, Queen of Scotland. James became the first ruler of England, Wales and Scotland.

Scotland and England continued to have separate Parliaments until 1707 when the Act of Union was passed. As a result of the Act, one Parliament was to govern the two countries. Many early monarchs had refused to co-operate with Parliament. By the time the Act of Union was agreed, the monarch had, more or less, handed over the running of the country to Parliament. Before an Act of Parliament can become law, it has to receive the monarch's approval. This is known as the Royal Assent. Queen Anne was the last monarch to refuse to give her assent to an Act of Parliament, in 1708 when she vetoed a Bill to reorganize the Scottish militia.

When Queen Anne died, the throne passed to the Elector of Hanover who came to Britain where he was crowned George I. Queen Elizabeth II is his great-great-great-great-great-great-great-granddaughter.

When, as is likely, Prince Charles accedes to the throne, he will be the nineteenth ruler of the United Kingdom.

THE SAXON & WARRIOR KINGS

About AD410 the Roman empire gave up its provinces of Britain, telling the British that they could not protect them from invaders from the Low Countries and Germany. We call the 300 years after the Romans left Britain the Dark Ages. We know little about the warrior kings who ruled the British Isles during this time.

ABOVE: The Angles, Saxons and Jutes divided England into the seven kingdoms shown on this map, with a ruler in charge of each part.

The first tales of a British warrior king called Arthur come from the Dark Ages. He is said to have led the struggle against the invaders for some years, but was killed at the Battle of Camlann in 537.

Three hundred years later, one king had become more powerful than all the others. He was King Egbert of Wessex. By 829, he forced the rulers of the other kingdoms to acknowledge him as their leader. Six years later, the Danes began coastal raids on England.

King Egbert fought against them and succeeded in driving them away for a time. When he died, his son Ethelwulf became King of Wessex. Ethelwulf had five sons. Amazingly, four of them became kings after him. His crown passed first to Ethelbald, who died in 858, then to Ethelbert, who lived for a further five years, and then his brother, Ethelred.

Ethelred had constant trouble with the Danes. In 865, the Danes invaded and occupied the kingdom of East Anglia. The following year, they ravaged Northumbria, and in 870 attacked Wessex. They were driven back by Ethelred and his young brother Alfred, who became king when Ethelred died in April 871.

Alfred was a brilliant leader, but the Danes were a formidable enemy. In January 878, they attacked his palace and

c. (about) AD450
The symbol for zero is invented by Indian mathematicians.

644–656
The complete text of the Qur'an, the Holy Book of Islam, is first written down.

696
Playing cards first appear in China. Fifty years later, the Chinese invent the first mechanical clock.

drove him out. He quickly formed a new army, however, and defeated the Danes only five months later at Edington, in Wiltshire. The Danes agreed to leave Wessex alone and retreated to East Anglia. When Alfred died in 899, his son Edward became King of Wessex. Edward was a real warrior, determined to make the Danes in England submit to his rule. By the time he died, he ruled over Wessex, Mercia, East Anglia, and Northumbria. His son, King Athelstan, added Yorkshire to his realm.

The most remarkable thing about Athelstan's successor, Edmund, was that he was stabbed to death while arresting an uninvited guest at a feast in 946.

Eadred, next on the throne, defeated the Norsemen who had invaded Northumbria. Then came Eadwig, who was only fifteen when he became king in 955.

Only four years later the crown passed to Edgar. By the time he came to the throne, the Wessex kings had established their supremacy over most of England.

King Edgar was the first king to be crowned ruler of all the English, at a special service at Bath Abbey in 973.

ABOVE: Ethelred and his younger brother, Alfred, fought back against the Danes and drove them off their lands after several skirmishes and battles near Reading.

BELOW: After his coronation, Edgar was rowed in a barge along the River Dee by eight kings of England and Scotland, as a token that they accepted him as their king.

800	c. 929	930
Charlemagne, King of France, creates a huge empire and is crowned Holy Roman Emperor by the Pope.	Good King Wenceslas – the Christian ruler of Bohemia – is murdered by his pagan brother.	Vikings discover Greenland. They sail from Iceland and, after they visit Greenland, they sail on to Newfoundland.

LAST OF THE SAXON KINGS

Edward the Martyr (975-978)

Edward was only thirteen when he became king on the death of his father, King Edgar. His stepmother Queen Elfrida had wanted the throne for her own son, Ethelred. She plotted for three years before inviting Edward to Corfe Castle in Dorset where he was murdered by her servants.

BELOW: The story of King Cnut tells that he loathed the way many of his subjects toadied to him, so he took a chair to the beach, sat on it and told the waves not to splash his feet. His wet feet proved to his courtiers that there was a limit to his authority!

Ethelred II (978-1013 and 1014-1016)

In 994 the King of Norway and the son of the King of Denmark sailed their longboats up the River Thames at the head of the largest Viking army seen in England for fifty years. Ethelred bought them off with a huge amount of gold. His nickname, 'the Unready', doesn't mean that he was unprepared, but that he was badly advised. In 1013, King Sweyn of Denmark invaded England. Ethelred fled to Normandy in northern France, while Sweyn ruled England. Ethelred thus gained another nickname, 'Ethelred the Exile'. When Sweyn died a year later, the English asked Ethelred to return.

Edmund II (1016)

Ethelred's son Edmund reigned for less than a year. The Danes, led by Sweyn's son Cnut, had invaded again in 1015. They defeated Edmund and forced him to divide England in two. Cnut took the lion's share, leaving Wessex to Edmund.

Cnut (1016-1035)

When Edmund II died, Cnut became king of all England. When his father Sweyn died in 1014, he also became King of Denmark; finally, there was peace between the two countries after many years of bitter war.

Harold I (1035-1040)

Before Cnut died he named his son Harthacnut as his heir. He was in Denmark, unable to claim his throne.

950
Maori navigators from Polynesia discover New Zealand.

 987
Hugh Capet becomes the first of a long line of kings of France which will reign for many centuries.

 c. 990
Cahokia, North America's first major city, is built near what is now St Louis and has 40,000 people living there.

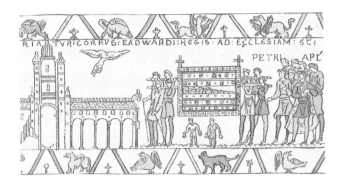

ABOVE: In 1065, Edward the Confessor ordered that a great church be built in London. He died before it was completed, but it still stands – Westminster Abbey, in London. His bones are buried there.

Some English noblemen suggested that his brother, Harold, should rule England in the meantime. Harold agreed, but once he was in control he had himself declared king and ruled for five years until he died.

Harthacnut (1040-1042)

When Harold died, Harthacnut sailed to England but became so despised that when he collapsed and died unexpectedly, there were few tears shed for him.

Edward the Confessor (1042-1066)

Edward, the son of Ethelred II, now came to the throne. He was a pious, saintly man, hence his nickname, 'the Confessor'.

The twenty-four years of his reign were mercifully peaceful except for a violent feud with Godwin, Earl of Wessex, over who should succeed him as king.

Harold II (1066)

Edward died childless. There were three people with strong claims to the English throne: William, the Duke of Normandy, who had been promised the throne by Edward; Harold, son of Godwin; and Harald Hardrada (Harald Fairhair), ruler of Norway.

Harold was in England when Edward died, while the others were overseas. William and Harald Hardrada invaded England. Harold defeated the Norsemen in Yorkshire, then marched his army south to Hastings in Sussex to do battle with William.

The armies met on 14 October 1066 near Hastings, where Harold was struck by an arrow and killed.

BELOW: The Battle of Hastings. Luckily for William, after Harold was killed, his soldiers took to their heels and fled, for had they stayed to fight, the dead king's men may well have won the battle.

1030	1035	1065
A medical school is built in Italy, but the doctors had to learn from Arab and Jewish doctors, who were much more skilled.	When Cnut dies, his empire of England, Norway and Denmark is split up into separate kingdoms.	The first known stained-glass window is placed in Augsburg Cathedral, in Germany.

WILLIAM THE CONQUEROR
& THE NORMAN KINGS

ABOVE: One of William's great loves was hunting. He created a huge forest in Hampshire which he stocked with deer. He called it the New Forest.

William the Conqueror (1066-1087)

After his victory at the Battle of Hastings, William became king.

The lands of the Saxon lords were confiscated and given to Norman noblemen.

William was keen to know exactly what his new kingdom contained, so he had a list drawn up of every city, town, village and hamlet, the people who lived there and the livestock they owned. This list became known as the Domesday Book.

William II (1087-1100)

The Conqueror was succeeded by his son, William. Although he was an excellent soldier and gained control of Normandy in France from his elder brother, Robert, he was hugely unpopular in England.

In 1100 he was hunting in the New Forest when he was killed by an arrow. His body was taken to Winchester and buried directly below the main tower in the Cathedral. The following year, the tower collapsed on his tomb.

Henry I (1100-1135)

William had no children. As soon as his brother, Henry, heard the news of his death he marched on Winchester and seized the royal treasury there. He was later crowned king. The other claimant to the throne was his elder brother, Robert, who had inherited Normandy when William the Conqueror died.

Robert was on a Crusade in the Holy Land when William II was killed. When he returned, his army was defeated by Henry in 1106. Henry was a particularly harsh, strict, methodical man, held in awe by his subjects. But he was wise and well educated, and governed England extremely well.

Stephen (1135-1154)

When Henry died, the true heir to the throne was his daughter, Matilda. But it was Henry's nephew who was crowned king, because some of the powerful barons did not want to be ruled by a woman.

1067
Work begins on the Bayeux Tapestry which tells the story of the Norman Conquest of England by the Duke of Normandy.

1088
One of Europe's first universities is founded at Bologna in Italy. Students and teachers alike must speak Latin.

1095
Pope Urban proclaims a Crusade against the Infidels to bring Jerusalem under Christian rule.

In 1138, Matilda's husband Geoffrey of Anjou invaded Stephen's territories in Normandy. In 1139, Stephen's troops captured Matilda. The King refused to have her imprisoned as he thought that would be unchivalrous. Matilda had no such scruples when, two years later, her troops captured Stephen. Matilda travelled to London for her coronation.

She was never crowned queen. Her high-and-mighty ways upset so many people that, when Stephen's troops advanced on the capital, Londoners took up arms and drove Matilda out.

The civil war lapsed into stalemate in 1144 after Geoffrey of Anjou invaded Normandy and was proclaimed duke.

The powerful English barons, many of whom held lands in Normandy, were reluctant to offend the new duke or his wife, and they persuaded Stephen to declare Matilda's son, Henry, as heir to the throne.

ABOVE: Henry I seized the royal treasury days after he heard William II was dead. He had to act quickly as his elder brother, Robert, was the true heir to the throne. Fortunately for Henry, Robert was in the Holy Land on a Crusade when William was killed.

ABOVE: Henry II appointed his old friend, Thomas Becket, as Archbishop of Canterbury, hoping to bring the Church under his authority. But when Becket sided with the Church, Henry was furious. One night he looked around his knights and said, 'Will no one rid me of this turbulent priest?' Some of the knights did just that and murdered Becket when he was in his cathedral in Canterbury.

Henry II (1154-1189)

Henry was rough, tough and clever – the complete opposite of Stephen. He forced the Scots out of England and invaded north Wales.

Henry's wife, Eleanor of Aquitaine, was a proud, fiery woman who came to dislike her husband so much that in 1173 she encouraged two of her sons, Henry and Richard, to take up arms against him!

A truce of sorts was reached, but Henry's refusal to let his sons share in his power eventually infuriated Richard and his brother John. In 1188, when King Philip of France declared war on Henry, the two English princes joined forces with him. Henry died shortly afterwards, a broken-hearted man.

1096
Crusaders return from the Holy Land with new foods including rice, sugar and lemons.

c. 1150–1450
The Kingdom of Great Zimbabwe flourishes, a major centre for work in gold, copper and iron.

1171
Henry II visits Ireland and receives submission from the Anglo-Norman lords and the Irish chieftains. He is accepted as Lord of Ireland.

RICHARD THE LIONHEART & KING JOHN

Richard I (1189-1199)

Henry II's son Richard I was known as 'the Lionheart' because he was so brave in battle. For three years of his reign he was on a Crusade in the Holy Land.

To raise money for his Crusade, Richard sold land, manors, earldoms – almost anything he could – to the highest bidder! He appointed William Longchamp, Bishop of Ely, to rule England while he was out of the country. But scarcely had he left the land than his ambitious brother, John, began to meddle. Within a few months, John was effectively ruling England.

With Richard away, and with Prince John's backing, many of the barons became very powerful. These harsh, cruel men treated the peasants who lived on their lands as little better than slaves. Some rebelled, and became outlaws. On the way back from the Crusade, King Richard was captured by the Duke of Austria, then held prisoner for almost a year and a half by the German Emperor, Henry VI, a former ally.

He returned to England only after a huge ransom had been paid, but a few months later he was off again, to defend his French territories which were under

ABOVE: For three years, Richard was fighting in the Holy Land which was under the control of the Turks. Richard and other European rulers made it their Crusade to return Jerusalem to Christian rule.

attack. He died in France, in 1199, after being injured by a bolt from a crossbow while laying siege to the castle of Chalus, in France.

John (1199-1216)

Richard had no children. The strongest claims to the throne belonged to Prince John, and his young nephew Arthur.

1190
The Angkor Empire is at the height of its power in Cambodia. The last of a magnificent series of temples is built.

c. 1200
Arab numbers instead of Roman numerals appear in Europe.

c. 1210
The first Christmas carols are written.

ABOVE: Richard received better treatment from his enemy, Saladin, leader of the Muslims, than he did from his allies. When the king's horse was killed in battle, Saladin sent him two magnificent Arab horses.

BELOW: In 1215, King John sealed the Magna Carta at Runnymede. It set out the rights of the barons, the Church and the citizens of England, including the right of all free Englishmen to a trial before they could be imprisoned.

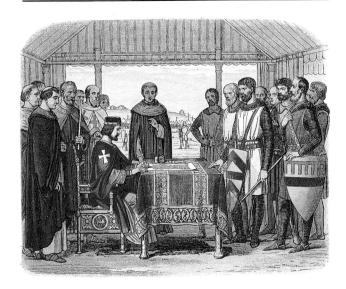

John gained the backing of the noblemen who did not want to be ruled by a boy. A few years later Arthur mysteriously disappeared and although there was no evidence, most people assumed that he'd been murdered on John's orders.

John ruled like a tyrant over his barons, who came to loathe him.

His foreign policies brought England into war with France. The barons might have forgiven him had he been victorious in battle, but he only succeeded in losing almost all of his father's huge empire in France.

In 1215 the English barons wrote a list of demands – the Magna Carta. Although John sealed it, many of the barons still did not trust him and invited Prince Louis of France to take the English throne.

The civil war that followed raged until, in October 1216, John became ill!. He tried to cheer himself up with a meal of peaches and cider, but this made him worse. A few days later he died and was buried at Worcester Cathedral, where his tomb can still be seen.

1210
The Pope approves the new Franciscan order of Friars, founded by Francis of Assisi. Members take a vow of poverty.

1210
Genghis Khan begins his conquest of China, then conquers Afghanistan, Iran, and southern Russia.

1212
Thousands of children set off for the Holy Land on a Crusade. Most of those who do not die on the way will be captured and sold into slavery.

THE PLANTAGENETS

Henry III (1216-1272)

On John's death, the throne passed to his nine-year-old son, Henry. A regency of churchmen and barons ruled on his behalf until, in 1227, Henry came of age.

He insisted on appointing his own counsellors. He spent vast amounts of money trying to regain lost lands in France. To pay for this, he simply raised taxes whenever he wanted to.

In 1263, the barons, led by Simon de Montfort, forced Henry to agree to mend his ways, but the King broke his word and the barons went to war.

They defeated Henry's army at the Battle of Lewes in 1264.

Henry became king in name only. De Montfort really ruled the land, but the other barons soon became jealous of his power. Led by Henry's son, Prince Edward, they rose against him.

Henry regained his throne, but it was Edward who took over the government of the country.

Edward I (1272-1307)

Edward I, Henry III's son, was good-looking, strong, a brilliant soldier and a wise king. He made himself popular with his subjects by stamping out corruption. His great ambition was to extend his rule to Wales and Scotland. By 1283, he had conquered Wales.

The Scots proved much more difficult to conquer. Though his many victories over them earned him the nickname 'Hammer of the Scots', he failed to subdue the country.

He died, aged sixty-eight, on his way to yet another campaign against the Scots.

Edward II (1307-1327)

Edward II could hardly have been more different from his father. Where his father listened to his advisers, Edward depended on the advice of his favourites such as his friends Piers Gaveston and Hugh Despenser.

LEFT: Edward I's son was born at Caernarvon Castle in Wales. Later, the King presented him to the people of Wales as their prince. The ceremony has been repeated many times as future monarchs presented their eldest sons to the Welsh people as Prince of Wales. Prince Charles became Prince of Wales in 1969.

1234
Mongol soldiers destroy most of the Chinese Empire. Kublai Khan, grandson of Genghis Khan, becomes Emperor of China in 1260.

1250
Italian traders found banks to look after Crusaders' money and start an early system of bank cheques.

1271
Marco Polo begins his journey to China, where he will serve Kublai Khan for seventeen years.

Edward's wife was the formidable Isabella of France. She loathed both Gaveston and Despenser. In 1325 she went to France to join forces with the King's enemies. Her army attacked Britain. The King was banished to Berkeley Castle in Gloucestershire where he was later most brutally murdered.

Edward III (1327-1377)

Edward III was fourteen when his father was killed. Until he came of age, the country was ruled by Isabella and her lover, Roger Mortimer. Through Isabella, Edward had a strong claim to the French throne, and he decided to fight for it. With his son, the Black Prince, Edward led the English army to a famous victory at Crécy in 1346. The English also captured Calais.

At home, he was popular with his barons. His armies defeated the Scots, and it looked as if the country was in for a period of peace and prosperity.

But then things changed. The French won back most of the territory the English had conquered. Edward grew old and confused. He quarrelled with his Parliament. The Black Prince died in 1376. A year later, Edward, a broken, shambling old man, followed him to the grave.

ABOVE: In 1348, the Black Death swept through England, killing one in every three people. This caused an enormous labour shortage and acute social unrest, leading to the Peasants' Revolt under Wat Tyler in 1381. Serfdom gradually declined from this date.

Richard II (1377-1399)

When Edward died, the Black Prince's son, ten-year-old Richard, became king. Government of the country was entrusted to a group of twelve men led by his uncle, John of Gaunt, Duke of Lancaster.

Richard believed that as king he had been appointed by God and could do whatever he liked. He offended the powerful noblemen including John of Gaunt whose son, Henry Bolingbroke, was banished.

When John of Gaunt died, his lands were seized by Richard. Bolingbroke sailed from Boulogne to claim them.

People flocked to Bolingbroke's side. Richard submitted to him at Flint in 1399.

He renounced the throne and Parliament appointed Bolingbroke his successor. Richard was sent to Pontefract Castle, where he is said to have been starved to death in 1400.

1309–1354
The main part of the magnificent Alhambra Palace in Granada in Spain is built by the Sultan Mohammed.

1348
Giovanni de Dondi, an Italian, makes a clock with seven faces to show the movement of the Sun, Moon and the five planets then known.

1368
The Ming dynasty begins in China, and becomes noted for the production of beautiful porcelain and art.

THE PRINCES OF WALES

From 410 until the Norman Conquest in 1066, Wales was divided into small states, each ruled by a tribal leader or king. Sometimes one king became stronger than the others, and would conquer the whole country, but he never ruled for very long.

BELOW: Llewelyn was eventually killed in a skirmish against the English. His head was cut off and taken to the Tower of London where it was stuck atop a pikestaff for all to see.

The situation changed after the Norman Conquest. The Norman barons moved into south Wales and over the next 200 years gradually took control. But they couldn't conquer the mountains of Snowdonia in the north. The area remained Welsh up to the thirteenth century, when the area was ruled over by Llewelyn, Prince of Wales.

In 1277 Edward I of England decided to bring Wales into his realm. His army invaded Wales and by the winter he had forced the Welsh to make peace. But the following spring, Llewelyn's army swept down from the hills again and captured several English castles.

Edward knew his troops could never cope with the steep mountains of Snowdonia, so he hired soldiers from the rugged Basque region of Spain to fight for him. But even they were no match for the Welsh. The war carried on until, when Llewelyn was occupied elsewhere, his army was defeated by the English. Llewelyn managed to rally his soldiers, but he was killed during a skirmish with the English in 1282.

In 1284 the Statute of Wales was passed, under which Wales fell to English rule. To reinforce his authority, Edward had nine huge castles built at strategic points throughout North Wales such as Harlech, Conway and Caernarvon. He manned them with his troops.

In 1301 he made his son, also called

c. 450–600		c. 613		c. 634
After Saxon conquerors drive the Celts out of much of their territory, the area we now call Wales becomes the main stronghold of the Celts.		Ethelfrith of Northumbria defeats the Celts at the Battle of Chester. The Saxons begin to refer to them as 'Wealas', the Saxon word for 'foreigner'.		Cadwallon, the Welsh leader, and his men are defeated in battle south of the River Tyne. The victorious English establish themselves in the foothills of the Welsh mountains.

Edward, the Prince of Wales, in a ceremony held at Caernarvon.

In 1400 a descendant of Llewelyn, Owen Glendower, fell into dispute with an English noble, Lord Grey, over some of Glendower's land which Grey had taken – King Henry IV could do nothing to force Grey to hand it back.

This squabble between neighbours turned into a full-scale rebellion. Welshmen flocked to join Glendower to throw the English out of Wales. For a while the Welsh had the upper hand, but in 1403, Glendower and his ally, Henry Percy, better known as Hotspur, were defeated by the English at the Battle of Shrewsbury. Two years later, the French sent troops to help Glendower in his fight, but although there were countless skirmishes, the English never looked in serious danger of losing control of Wales.

ABOVE: When Henry IV refused to intervene in Glendower's squabble with Grey, the Welshman took the law into his own hands, drove Grey off his lands and put the town of Ruthyn to the torch.

ABOVE: Hotspur's death at the Battle of Shrewsbury.

c. 785
Offa, the King of Mercia, the most powerful man in England, builds a great earthwork to mark the boundary between England and Wales. Parts of Offa's Dyke can still be seen today.

878
Rhodri the Great dies. He had ruled most of the country and had successfully beaten off attacks from Scandinavian sea-raiders.

c. 909–949
Hywel the Good establishes himself as master of most of Wales. Although he introduces many good laws, he acknowledges the supremacy of King Athelstan of England.

15

THE LANCASTRIANS

Henry IV (1399-1413)

Having seized the throne from Richard II, the dashing, romantic and chivalrous Henry Bolingbroke, the first Lancastrian King, found it was not easy to hold on to it. He had to contend with the Welsh, continue the wars in France and cope with the Scots. Within a matter of months of ousting Richard, he discovered that the English nobles were plotting against him.

The most dangerous challenge came from the Duke of Northumberland and his son Hotspur (Henry Percy). They owned much of Northumberland, and were constantly having to fight off attacks from the Scots to the north - a costly business for which they considered the King should reward them. His refusal led to civil war and Hotspur's death at the Battle of Shrewsbury.

The years of Henry's reign are marked by constant revolts against his rule which Henry put down quite ruthlessly. In 1400, when thirty rebels were horribly executed, their drawn and quartered bodies were displayed in London as a warning to others. In 1405, the Archbishop of York was executed for his part in another plot against the King.

Henry was constantly plagued with guilt over his treatment of Richard. Whatever his faults, Richard had been rightful king. There were others, the children of his father's older brother, the Duke of Clarence, with better claims to the throne.

ABOVE: Henry IV was crowned on 13th October 1399. Three months later he had to flee from Windsor to London to escape a plot backed by supporters of Richard II. The rebel leaders were eventually captured and beheaded.

Henry died a bitter, confused, sick man. All his life he suffered from headlice and chronic eczema. By the time he died, his face and body were badly disfigured.

Years after his death, his Uncle Clarence's descendants would identify themselves with the Yorkists in the Wars of the Roses, the seeds of which were sown when Henry Bolingbroke usurped the throne of its rightful occupant.

Henry V (1413-1422)

Henry IV was succeeded by his son, Henry V, a young, clever, gifted man – a great soldier who was popular with the people.

1369–1405
Tamerlane, a descendant of Genghis Khan, conquers a huge empire which stretches from Mongolia to the Mediterranean.

1401
After the Catholic Church issues a statute on the burning of heretics (men and women who refuse to follow the Catholic faith), many followers of religious reformer John Wycliffe are burned at the stake.

1403
Yung Lo, a Chinese scholar, compiles an encyclopedia in 22,937 volumes. Only three copies are made.

He was shrewd enough to know that one way of ensuring his subjects' loyalty and to stop his noblemen plotting against him was to unite them in a war against France.

Henry had a reasonable claim to the French throne, and in 1415, at the head of a large army, he set off to conquer France. He won a famous victory at the Battle of Agincourt where his archers rained arrows on the French knights, bogged down in the mud by the heavy armour they wore. Four years later, he returned to France and regained Normandy for the English crown.

He looked more like a monk than a soldier, with his sombre brown eyes, pursed lips and overlong nose. He was a devout Christian and a glutton for hard work.

BELOW: On 25 October 1415, Henry V led his men into battle against the French at Agincourt, in northern France. English archers rained arrows on to the French, killing nearly 1,500 knights.

ABOVE: After his coronation, Henry V made peace with many noblemen who had suffered during his father's reign. He also had Richard II's body taken from its grave and reburied in Westminster Abbey.

In 1421, he laid siege to Meaux, a French stronghold in the Loire Valley. The town fell in 1422. It was Henry's last triumph. Later that year, he fell ill and died, without having realized his great ambition of sitting on the French throne.

1404
The Welsh enter into an alliance with the French. A year later, French troops land to support a rebellion against the English which eventually ends in defeat.

1405–1433
Cheng Ho, a Chinese explorer, travels to India, Iran and Africa, and opens up trade between them and China.

c. 1420
The Portuguese, led by Prince Henry the Navigator, start exploring West Africa. This will lead to the development of the gold, ivory and slave trades.

LEFT: In 1420, Charles VI of France and Henry V signed the Treaty of Troyes which recognized Henry as heir to the French throne. Henry married Charles's daughter, Catherine, but his new brother-in-law, the Dauphin, refused to recognize Henry as heir.

were to afflict him throughout his life. Richard, Duke of York, was appointed Protector of England. As a descendant of Lionel, Duke of Clarence (Edward III's third son), the Duke of York had a stronger claim to the throne than Henry who was descended from John, Duke of Lancaster (Edward III's fourth son).

York and Queen Margaret despised each other, and when Henry had recovered his sanity, she persuaded her husband to dismiss the Duke. The Duke's response was to gather an army which met the King's troops at the Battle of St Albans in 1455.

Henry VI (1422-1461 and 1470-1471)

Henry VI was only nine months old when his father, Henry V, died and he became the youngest king England has ever had. He was crowned King of England when he was nearly eight and King of France when he was ten. His uncles governed until he was old enough to do so.

As a youth, he spied on his servants, in case any of them smuggled a woman into their rooms! He was so pious that on feast days when, by tradition, he wore his crown, he wore an itchy hair shirt next to his skin as penance for the sin of pride.

In 1445, Henry married the strong-minded French princess, Margaret of Anjou. Eight years later, he was to suffer the first of many bouts of insanity that

ABOVE: Henry VI was responsible for the founding of Eton College, in 1440. His statue can be seen in School Yard there.

1431

Joan of Arc is burned at the stake for witchcraft, by the English. She will eventually be made a saint – in 1920.

c. 1450

German goldsmith Johann Gutenberg invents a method of using movable type which can be used again and again. In 1455 he produces the Mazarin Bible, the first book to be printed in Europe.

1453

Constantinople is taken by the Turks and renamed Istanbul. The Turks establish themselves as leaders of the Muslim world and destroy many Christian states.

The Yorkists won the battle. The Duke of York forced Henry to forgive him his treason. A few months later, Henry was unwell again, and the Duke was again appointed Protector. A year later, Henry was sane enough to rule and tried to maintain peace between the two sides. But Margaret was determined to thwart York and do everything she could to ensure that her son, Edward, would one day inherit his father's throne.

She raised an army and defeated the Yorkists at Wakefield in 1460. The Duke of York was killed, but the following year, his followers defeated Margaret at the Battle of Towton. The Duke's son Edward was declared king and was crowned at Westminster Abbey as Edward IV.

Margaret refused to give up, but she was forced to flee to France with her son after being defeated in battle in 1463. Henry was eventually taken prisoner and thrown in the Tower in 1465.

Five years later, he was freed by the

ABOVE: Joan of Arc was a simple peasant girl who claimed she heard the voices of Saint Michael, Saint Katherine and Saint Margaret telling her to drive the English out of France. Clad in a suit of white armour, she led the Dauphin and an army of 12,000 men through English territory to Rheims where the Dauphin was crowned King of France. She was later taken prisoner, sold to the English for 10,000 crowns, and burned at the stake as a witch.

powerful Earl of Warwick who turned traitor against his cousin, Edward IV, and allied his troops with Margaret's.

With the Yorkists in disarray, Warwick restored Henry to the throne. But not for long. In 1471, Edward routed Warwick's army at Barnet, and Margaret's at Tewkesbury, where she was taken prisoner and her son died.

Edward marched back to London and on the night he arrived, Henry VI – a sad old man who had lost his mind, two kingdoms and his son – was quietly murdered.

1453
More than 100 years of war against France come to an end when the French succeed in driving England out of their country. The only English territory in France is Calais, on the English Channel.

1464
Sunni Ali becomes ruler of the huge Songhai Empire in West Africa, and begins to trade across the Sahara Desert.

1465

Printed music first appears in Europe.

THE HOUSE OF YORK

LEFT: Richard of York's emblem was a white rose. The Lancastrians adopted a red rose as their symbol. The Battle of Saint Albans was the first of the twelve battles and countless skirmishes that came to be called 'The Wars of the Roses'. If you look closely at a 20 pence coin, you can see the two roses.

Edward IV (1461-1470 and 1471-1483)

When Richard of York's son, Edward, Earl of March, was declared king in 1461, the English were well pleased, for he was tall, handsome, brave, charming and popular. After the struggles against Warwick and Margaret of Anjou, and with Henry VI and his son both dead, Edward felt secure on the throne. Trade with Europe was revived and England became prosperous again. Edward was a skilled businessman and amassed a huge fortune from his own trading deals. Edward loved to be seen in public wearing the latest fashions, and treated all his subjects – baron or baker – with the same outgoing friendliness.

Edward died of a fever in 1483, the first king for many generations not to die in debt! He willed that the crown pass to his son, Prince Edward, and that until he came of age, his brother, Richard, Duke of Gloucester, should be Protector.

Edward V (1483)

Edward V is at the centre of one of the biggest mysteries in English history. He was 12 years old when his uncle took him to London for his coronation.

While Edward was waiting to be crowned, the Bishop of Bath and Wells suggested that his parents may not have been properly married. That made young Edward illegitimate, and an illegitimate child could not inherit the crown.

Edward was deposed and the throne offered to Richard, who was crowned king in July 1483. After August that year, neither Edward nor his young brother, the Duke of York, were ever seen again! Popular folklore has it that the two boys were smothered to death as they slept, on the orders of Richard. We shall probably never know the truth.

Richard III (1483-1485)

In Shakespeare's play, *Richard III*, Richard is portrayed as a wicked hunchback who commits murder without

---

1467
The barons of Japan begin a civil war that will last over a hundred years.

1469
The marriage of Ferdinand of Aragon and Isabella of Castille unites Spain as one country.

1471 onwards
Portuguese explorers establish trading posts in Africa from Tunis in the north to Angola and Mozambique in the south.

ABOVE: In 1478 Edward IV's brother, the Duke of Clarence, was accused of treason and found guilty. Edward could have shown mercy, but he allowed his brother to be executed. Tradition has it that Clarence was drowned in a butt of Malmsey wine.

a second thought. But most of the evidence shows that Richard was, in fact, an honest person, a good administrator, an able soldier and a faithful husband. How did this change of image happen?

Richard was a Yorkist. The Lancastrians were now led by Henry Tudor, a great-great grandson of John of Gaunt, and a grandson of Henry V's widow who had married Owen Tudor after her husband had died.

Although Edward IV's wife, Elizabeth Woodville, had been the wife of a Yorkist, she and Richard were long-standing enemies. She agreed that Henry Tudor should marry her daughter, Elizabeth. Such a marriage would unite two people, each with a claim to the throne.

War was inevitable. In 1485, Henry Tudor landed in South Wales. Two weeks later, the Lancastrian and Yorkist armies met for the last time. The battle took place at Bosworth, near Leicester. Richard was killed after leading a cavalry charge directed at Henry Tudor.

Now, back to our question. How did Richard acquire such a bad reputation? When Shakespeare wrote *Richard III* there was a Tudor queen, Elizabeth I, on the throne. Richard had been the enemy of the Tudors, so Shakespeare could not displease the Queen by showing Richard in a good light. Shakespeare's black portrait of Richard persisted and it is only in the last hundred years or so that historians have begun to discover something of the truth.

BELOW: Richard III at Bosworth. His crown was found in a bush after the Battle of Bosworth, and given to Henry Tudor.

1474
The Histories of Troy is printed by William Caxton's printing press in Bruges – the first book in English.

1478
The Spanish Inquisition is formed with the aim of destroying the Muslim and Jewish minorities in Spain.

1489
Plus and minus signs first begin to be used in mathematics.

THE TUDORS

Henry VII (1485-1509)

Henry Tudor's marriage to Elizabeth united the rival houses of Lancaster and York. Henry was an organized and careful man. He kept tight control over the Exchequer and amassed a large private fortune so that he would never have to ask Parliament for money.

A good diplomat and businessman, he was exactly the sort of king England needed at the time. He made trading treaties with European powers. His reign brought internal peace and prosperity.

Henry VIII (1509-1547)

Prince Henry had not expected to be king until his elder brother, Prince Arthur, died in 1502, a year after marrying Catherine of Aragon. Seven weeks after he came to the throne he married his brother's widow.

She gave birth to a daughter, Mary, in 1516, but the son needed to secure the Tudor succession had died in 1512, aged two months. Henry decided to divorce Catherine and find another wife. The Roman Catholic Church refused Henry's request for a divorce.

Henry's response was to break away from the Church in Rome. His second wife, Anne Boleyn, bore another daughter, Elizabeth, but no son and heir.

Eventually, Henry had her arrested on trumped-up charges of treason, and executed.

BELOW: Henry VIII was tall and handsome, outgoing, boisterously high-spirited, reckless with the money his father so carefully hoarded, and easily distracted by a pretty lady!

1488
Bartholomeu Dias reaches the Cape of Good Hope, the southern tip of Africa.

1492
Christopher Columbus lands in the Caribbean islands. Thinking that he has reached India, he calls them the West Indies.

1519
Hernan Cortez leads an army of 550 Spanish men into Mexico and conquers the vast Aztec Empire within two years.

His next wife was Jane Seymour. She gave birth to the son Henry so desperately wanted, but died soon afterwards. He next married on the advice of his ministers to cement an alliance with the Low Countries. It is said that he took one look at the plain, dumpy Anne of Cleves, who spoke no English at the time of their marriage, and decided to divorce her as soon as he could after they were married. His attention next turned to the beautiful Catherine Howard. Two years later, Catherine met the same fate as Anne Boleyn.

His last wife was a motherly figure, Catherine Parr. By the time they were married, Henry was fat and ill. Catherine cared for him until he died.

Edward VI (1547-1553)

Edward, Henry's only son, became king when he was ten years old. When he was fifteen, Edward became so seriously ill that it was obvious he would die. The next person in line to the throne was his sister Mary, a devout Roman Catholic. Edward was persuaded to name a Protestant cousin, Jane Grey, as his heir.

LEFT: In his later years, Henry became bloated and ugly. People who had not known him in his youth found it hard to believe that he had been a fine horseman, a keen jouster, an avid huntsman, a good dancer, a man of culture and knowledge – a true Renaissance prince.

Jane (July 1553)

Lady Jane Grey had no ambition to be queen. Mary Tudor rallied the people to her own standard and marched on London, where she was hailed as queen only nine days after Jane had been put on the throne.

Mary Tudor (1553-1558)

Mary was determined to make England a Catholic country again. She married a Catholic prince, Philip, the heir to the throne of Spain. In 1557, Philip persuaded Mary to join Spain in a war against France. It was a disaster. The following year, Mary died, unloved, unwanted and unsuccessful.

BELOW: Mary was so determined to restore the Catholic faith that Protestants were liable to be arrested. During her reign, three hundred of them were burned at the stake for refusing to become Roman Catholics.

1520	1534	1547
Henry VIII and Francis I of France meet at the Field of the Cloth of Gold in Flanders to conclude peace between their two countries.	Jacques Cartier is the first of several French explorers to reach Canada and begin to explore it.	Ivan of Russia styles himself Tsar or Emperor, and after his army is defeated by Poland begins a reign of terror that earns him the nickname 'Ivan the Terrible'.

23

ELIZABETH I

Elizabeth's cousin, Mary, Queen of Scots, who, as a devout Roman Catholic, considered herself to be the true Queen of England.

In 1568, Mary was forced to flee Scotland and throw herself on Elizabeth's mercy. The English Queen kept Mary under virtual house arrest for twenty years in one manor house after another.

The beautiful Scottish Queen became the focus of Catholic plots to depose Elizabeth, and put Mary on the throne in her place.

She was eventually taken to Fotheringhay Castle and charged with

Elizabeth came to the throne when Mary died in 1558. She heard the news when she was staying at Hatfield House to the north of London and rode triumphantly into the city as Queen Elizabeth of England. She made England a Protestant country again, but she did not treat the Catholics with the same cruelty that Mary had shown to her Protestant subjects.

The Queen was courted by foreign princes and English noblemen. She flirted with some and seemed serious with others. Her counsellors hoped that she would marry one of them and produce a male, Protestant, heir, but she never did.

The next in line to the throne was

BELOW: During the reign of her sister, Mary I, Elizabeth was for a while imprisoned in the Tower of London. Nothing could be proved against her and she was freed.

1556–1605
Akbar the Great rules India, and tries to unite Muslims and Hindus by allowing Hindus to practise their religion.

1562–1598
There are religious wars in France between Catholics and Protestants, until both are finally given equal rights.

c. 1565
The first wooden pencil with a graphite lead is invented in Switzerland.

treason. She was found guilty and sentenced to death. At first Elizabeth refused to sign her cousin's death warrant. For three months she wavered until in February 1587 she put her pen to the document. Mary was executed a few days later. Europe's Catholic monarchs were furious and this was one of the reasons why, the following year, Philip of Spain sent a huge fleet of ships, the Spanish Armada, to attack England.

The Armada was beaten by a combination of the brilliant tactics of the English fleet commanded by Lord Howard, Sir Francis Drake, Sir John Hawkins and Martin Frobisher, and ferocious weather.

During Elizabeth's reign, English captains sailed on voyages of discovery. Francis Drake became the first Englishman to sail round the world.

Although Elizabeth had no children, her subjects were relieved when she named a Protestant king as her heir – the son of Mary, Queen of Scots, James VI, who came to the throne when Elizabeth died in 1603, as James I of England.

ABOVE: Violent storms blew up which scattered the Armada. Many of its ships foundered as they sailed round Scotland on the homeward voyage to Cadiz.

ABOVE: Elizabeth was hugely popular with her subjects. She travelled round the country, visiting the homes of her favourite noblemen.

1568
The Dutch rebel against their Spanish rulers, and will eventually achieve independence eighty years later.

 1571
The battle of Lepanto, off the coast of Greece, ends the Turkish threat to Europe from the sea.

 c. 1590
The microscope is invented by Zacharias Janssen, a Dutch lens-maker.

THE KINGS & QUEENS OF SCOTLAND

LEFT: Mary, Queen of Scots with her husband, Lord Darnley. Darnley was so jealous of Mary's fondness for one of her musicians, David Rizzio, that he had him murdered before his wife's eyes.

Until 1603, Scotland had a royal history quite separate from that of England. Unlike the English and Welsh, the Scots were never conquered by the Romans. In ancient times, Scotland was split up into many kingdoms, but in 844 Kenneth MacAlpin became the first king of all Scotland.

MacAlpin's descendants occupied the throne until 1290 when the seven-year-old heir to the crown, Margaret, died on her voyage from Norway, where she had been living, to Scotland.

Thirteen people claimed the crown. Edward I of England, who was asked to choose one of them, selected John Balliol whom, he thought, would do what he was told by the English. In 1296 the Scots rebelled. Edward's response was to invade Scotland and imprison Balliol.

The struggle for independence was taken up by two Scottish heroes, Sir William Wallace and Robert Bruce. Wallace defeated Edward and invaded the northern counties of England, but in 1305 he was captured and brought to London, where he was executed at Smithfield.

One of the greatest of all Scottish leaders, Robert Bruce, was crowned Robert I in 1306. One by one he captured English strongholds until all but Stirling Castle were in his hands. When Bruce laid siege to it, in 1314, the governor asked Edward II for help. Edward marched north at the head of his troops and the two armies met at Bannockburn, near Stirling. The Scots won a famous victory that forced the English to accept once and for all that Scotland was an independent country.

In 1371 the Stewart family inherited the

1018
Malcolm II defeats the Northumbrians and adds the Lothians to his territory.

1040
Macbeth murders Duncan, King of Scotland, and takes the throne for himself.

1469
James III of Scotland marries Margaret of Norway. As part of her dowry Margaret brings the Orkney and Shetland Islands, which have been part of Scotland ever since.

throne. For two centuries their followers raided English estates just over the border, a continual thorn in the English side.

Perhaps the most famous Scottish monarch of all was Mary, Queen of Scots. She married the heir to the French throne, but returned to Scotland a young widow, in 1561. She then married Lord Darnley who was killed in 1567. It was believed that the Earl of Bothwell had murdered him – and

just a few months later, Mary married Bothwell. This was too much for the Scots. Mary was forced to abdicate and give the crown to her young son, James. She fled to England where, after being involved in plots against Elizabeth I, she was executed in 1587.

Eventually in 1603, after hundreds of years of war between the two countries, they were united peacefully. Elizabeth I, who had no children of her own, made James VI of Scotland, son of Mary, her heir. When she died James became king of both Scotland and England, and ever since that time the same monarch has ruled over both countries.

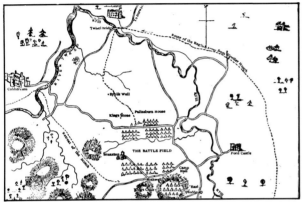

LEFT AND BELOW: In 1513, James IV of Scotland invaded England while Henry VIII was in France. The Scots were driven back and defeated by the English at the Battle of Flodden where James and many of his noblemen were killed.

1692
Many members of the Clan Macdonald are put to the sword by their enemies, the Campbells, in the Glencoe Massacre.

1715
The Scots rise up against the Hanoverian succession in the first Jacobite Rebellion. They want to put James II's son on the throne.

1745
Scots rally to Bonnie Prince Charlie – who vows to restore the throne to the Stuarts. The Scots march as far south as Derby before returning to Scotland, and defeat at the Battle of Culloden, in 1746.

THE HOUSE OF STUART

James I (1603-1625)

James became King of Scotland in 1567 when he was only one year old. In 1603, he inherited the English crown from Elizabeth I. His popularity waned when he promoted his friends, such as the Duke of Buckingham, to powerful posts.

BELOW: In 1605, a group of Roman Catholics including Guy Fawkes came close to blowing up Parliament while James was there. James was equally unpopular with the Puritans, extreme Protestants whom he angered by refusing to pass the religious reforms they wanted.

Parliament's objections were simply ignored by the high-and-mighty James.

James believed that kings had been ordained by God to rule. This was known as the Divine Right of Kings. He was constantly at odds with his Parliament and, indeed, ruled without them from 1614 to 1621.

He was extravagant, especially in the gifts he gave to his male favourites, and at one time was forced to borrow money from his wife's goldsmith. Although he was very intelligent, he liked nothing more than the sound of his own voice and earned himself the nickname, 'The Wisest Fool in Christendom'. He was said to be a very messy eater and had a bad stammer.

Charles I (1625-1649)

Charles was handsome, charming and a great patron of the arts. But, like his father, James I, he believed in the Divine Right of Kings and that no one had the right to question what he did. In 1629, when Parliament refused to grant him the money he asked for, he decided to rule without them and did so for eleven years.

To add to his unpopularity, his wife, Henrietta Maria, was a fervent Roman Catholic who encouraged him in his struggle against Parliament. But in 1640, he was forced to summon MPs to Westminster to raise more money.

Parliament reacted by demanding the

1607
Tea is first introduced into Europe from China by the Dutch.

 1619
Slaves from West Africa are used by the British in Virginia, a hundred years after Spain and Portugal first transported slaves to the Americas.

 1620
The Pilgrim Fathers, 102 men, women and children, set sail from Plymouth in the *Mayflower*. After a stormy crossing, they arrive in Massachusetts and establish a colony.

execution of Charles's chief minister, Lord Strafford, and by refusing to raise taxes. Charles responded by entering Parliament with armed soldiers to arrest the members who, in the King's opinion, were the chief troublemakers. The country became divided into two camps: those who supported the King (the Royalists), and those who sided with Parliament (the Parliamentarians).

Civil war erupted throughout the country. In 1645, Charles and his supporters, known as Cavaliers, were finally defeated by the Parliamentarian leader, Oliver Cromwell, at the Battle of Naseby. The King was brought to trial at Westminster in 1648 and condemned to death.

The Interregnum

From 1649 until 1658 England was a republic. Although he was a Parliamentarian, Cromwell was often at odds with his followers and had to use his army to impose changes. In 1653 his patience snapped. He dissolved Parliament, and made himself Lord Protector, with all the powers of a king. The Interregnum (meaning between two reigns) is known as the Commonwealth.

Cromwell's regime was strictly Puritan – he closed the theatres and insisted that everyone observed the Sabbath. Any frivolity was frowned upon.

When he was having his portrait painted, he insisted that the artist portray him as he really was – 'warts and all'.

When Cromwell died in 1658, his son Richard took over but resigned after only a few months. After weeks without a

ABOVE: Charles I was often painted on horseback. The reason was that he was very short, a fact that painters such as Van Dyck could disguise by depicting him riding.

leader, Parliament agreed to invite Charles I's eldest son to return and take the throne as Charles II.

1632–1653
Twenty thousand men are at work building the Taj Mahal in India, a memorial to Shah Jahan's favourite wife.

1642
Galileo Galilei dies. Galileo confirmed that the Earth orbits the Sun and was persecuted by the Catholic Church for saying so.

1649
In Russia, a law turns all peasants into serfs who can be bought and sold like slaves. Serfdom is to last for 200 years.

THE LATER STUARTS

Charles II (1660-1685)

The new king entered London on his thirtieth birthday. His dashing good looks and rollicking sense of humour made him popular with his subjects. Theatres reopened. Singing and dancing were allowed again.

Charles and his wife Catherine had no children of their own. The heir was Charles's brother James, a devout Catholic. Attempts by Protestants to ban James from the succession were always thwarted by Charles, who organized things so that when he died, the crown passed peacefully to his brother.

James II (1685-1688)

When he became king, James infuriated Parliament by appointing Catholics to the most important offices of state. He was tolerated because the next in line to the

ABOVE: After William died, the supporters of James II and his successors (the Jacobites) often drank the health of 'The gentleman in the black velvet waistcoat' – the mole over whose molehill William's horse had stumbled.

throne was his grown-up daughter, Mary, who was married to the Protestant Prince William of Orange. Things changed in 1688 when the Queen (James' second wife) gave birth to a son, who then became heir to the throne. In order to secure the Protestant succession, a group of conspirators sent a secret message to Mary's husband asking him to invade England.

James fled to France (his wife and son were already there), vowing that he would sit on the British throne again. He raised an army and landed in Ireland the following year. His men were beaten by

---

1669
The Mughal Emperor Aurangzeb orders local governors to destroy all non-Islamic temples and schools in India.

1670
Minute hands are used on watches for the first time.

1680
The last dodo, a flightless bird found on the island of Mauritius, is killed and the breed becomes extinct.

William's troops at the Battle of the Boyne, and James returned to France, never to set foot in England again.

William III and Mary II (1689-1702)

Though Mary was the true successor to James II, she had promised her husband, William of Orange, that if she ever came to the throne of England he could rule the country jointly with her. William and Mary were both rather serious, dull people. They submitted to the controls put on royal power that Parliament wanted. William ruled alone after Mary's death in 1694. In 1701, he made it impossible for a Roman Catholic ever to sit on the British throne again when he signed the Act of Settlement, which barred Catholics from the succession.

BELOW: Although Anne and her husband lacked sparkle, during her reign some of the most glittering men of British history flourished. They included (from L to R) Sir Christopher Wren whose buildings include St Paul's Cathedral in London; Isaac Newton, Master of the Royal Mint and one of Britain's greatest scientists; and John Churchill, Duke of Marlborough, who won several brilliant victories over the French army in Europe.

William died the following year, after his horse stumbled on a molehill and threw him to the ground.

Anne (1702-1714)

William and Mary had no children, so the throne passed to Mary's sister, Anne.

Queen Anne was the last of the Stuart monarchs. She was a kind, capable woman, more interested in playing cards and drinking tea than in affairs of state. One of the most important events of Anne's reign was the signing of the Act of Union in 1707. Although England and Scotland were ruled by the same monarch, they were governed by separate parliaments. The Act of Union changed this. England and Scotland become one United Kingdom.

1682
Robert la Salle claims the Mississippi and its valley for France, naming the area Louisiana after Louis XIV of France.

1685
Louis XIV bans all religions except Catholicism in France, and half a million Huguenots (Protestants) flee the country.

1698
Peter the Great of Russia begins a period of expansion and modernization of his country.

GEORGE I

Towards the end of her life, Queen Anne and Parliament had to decide who should rule Britain on her death. The Act of Settlement ruled out a Roman

Catholic, so it was decided to offer the throne to a granddaughter of James I and VI – the Electress Sophia of Hanover, in Germany. Sophia died a few weeks before Anne and it was Sophia's son, George, who became the first Hanoverian monarch of Britain.

The year after he took the throne, there was a rebellion aimed at restoring the Stuarts to the throne. The rebels, the Jacobites, were defeated and their leaders executed, but there was always a danger that the Jacobites would rise again. Little wonder, perhaps, that George spent long periods of his reign in Germany.

The country was now governed by a group of ministers in Parliament who were known as the cabinet. George's place was usually taken at cabinet meetings by a chief minister who eventually came to be known as the 'prime' minister.

Royalist and Puritan factions in Parliament had by now long given way

LEFT: George I. In his native Hanover, George was an absolute ruler: but in Britain, most of the monarch's power had passed to Parliament. George found this difficult to accept. He did not like the English, and did not bother to learn more than a few words of the language.

1703
Peter the Great begins to build the new city of St Petersburg, which becomes the capital of Russia in 1712.

 1714
Gabriel Fahrenheit, a German scientist, makes the first mercury thermometer with a temperature scale. The Fahrenheit Scale is still used in many parts of the world today.

 1716
The teaching of Christianity is prohibited in China.

to two main parties – the Whigs and the Tories (the forerunners of today's Liberal and Conservative parties). George was a great supporter of the Whigs and despised the Tories, whom he suspected of siding with the Jacobites. Robert Walpole, a Whig, became George's adviser and the most powerful man in the country. He is sometimes called Britain's first prime minister, though at the time there was no such official title.

George had divorced his wife twenty years before he acceded to the British throne. Not only that, he had her imprisoned until she died, in 1726, much

ABOVE: In 1715, the first Jacobite Rebellion was crushed by George I's soldiers. Thirty years later, the Scots rallied to Prince Charles Edward Stuart who progressed in triumph as far south as Derby before turning back. The two armies met at Culloden in 1746 where the Scots were beaten.

to the fury of their son, George II. Father and son loathed each other so deeply that at one point the king thought of having the prince kidnapped and taken to America to get him out of the way! But there was nothing he could do to prevent George taking the throne on his death, which happened while he was travelling to Hanover in 1727.

1717
School attendance is made compulsory in Prussia.

1721
Russian factory owners are allowed to buy peasants, who are then forced to work virtually as slaves in their factories.

1725
The Italian composer Vivaldi writes *The Four Seasons*. Altogether, he wrote over 400 concertos.

GEORGE II & 'FARMER GEORGE'

George II (1727-1760)

George II was much more easy-going than his father, and even if he did interfere in government much more than him, at least he spoke English – albeit with a heavy German accent.

In 1742, Britain went to war in Europe and during the campaigns that followed, George led his army in battle, at Dettingen in 1743 – the last British king to do so. In other parts of the world, George's armies enjoyed some splendid victories. Clive's defeat of the French in India in 1757 eventually resulted in India's becoming part of the British Empire, and two years later, Canada was added to Britain's overseas territories when General Wolfe took Quebec from France.

George III (1760-1820)

George II was succeeded not by his eldest son, Frederick Louis, Prince of Wales, who had died before his father, but by Frederick's son, who became George III. His deep interest in the changes that happened in agriculture during his reign

BELOW: Although George III preferred to live in Windsor or Kew, in 1762 he bought Buckingham House (now Buckingham Palace), near St James's Park in the heart of London.

1764		1773		1789
Mozart, the great Austrian composer, writes his first symphony at the age of eight.		American settlers disguised as Indians attack British ships in Boston Harbour. The Boston Tea Party is one of the sparks that leads to the American War of Independence.		Parisians storm the Bastille, a prison in Paris, thus beginning the French Revolution, during which the King, Queen and thousands of aristocrats are executed.

earned him the nickname, 'Farmer George'. These changes, known as the Agricultural Revolution, made farming much more efficient.

Another great change was the loss of the American colonies, the oldest part of the British Empire. In 1773, some colonists, disguised as Indians, attacked British ships in Boston Harbour and poured their cargoes of tea into the water. They did this to protest about the fact that although they were taxed by the British, they were not represented in Parliament. The incident became known as 'The Boston Tea Party', and eventually led to the War of Independence.

In 1764 the King suffered his first attack of madness, probably brought about by an illness called porphyria, which affects the brain and the nervous system. Though he recovered, he suffered further and more serious attacks.

ABOVE: During George's reign, James Watt designed an efficient steam engine. This was one of the machines that led to the Industrial Revolution that eventually made Britain the strongest power in Europe and the world.

George was a family man, never happier than when surrounded by his wife and children, although the escapades of his son, the Prince of Wales, were a constant concern. The King was immensely popular with the people. Part of this popularity was due to the naval and military successes of Lord Nelson and the Duke of Wellington in the wars against Napoleon.

In 1811, four years before the wars finally ended, the King suffered his worst and longest attack of insanity. Blind, deaf and mad, he spent his last years at Windsor Castle while the son he disliked so much, the Prince of Wales, ruled as Prince Regent.

1792		1804		1815
Denmark becomes the first country to ban the slave trade.		Napoleon crowns himself Emperor of France. Within eight years, France controls most of Europe, but he makes a mistake in 1812 when French troops march on Russia.		The Duke of Wellington defeats Napoleon at the Battle of Waterloo. The outcome may well have been different if Prussian troops had not arrived in time.

GEORGE IV &
—THE SAILOR KING—

George IV (1820-1830)

In contrast to his careful, quiet father, George was a wild, rebellious young man whose fondness for clothes, women, gambling, drinking and horse-racing was the talk of London's clubs and coffee houses.

His behaviour drove the King to despair, but Prince George did not care. It also did not concern him that he was becoming unpopular with the people.

There was a great deal of poverty in Britain at the time. The war with France was costly and was financed with high taxes. Many people resented George's extravagance, so much so that there were several attempts on his life!

In 1820 George III died and George, the Prince Regent, became George IV. His magnificent coronation was marred by the unexpected arrival of his wife, Queen Caroline, who was unceremoniously locked out of Westminster Abbey.

His attempts to divorce the Queen were stopped only by her death in 1821. His treatment of her made him even more unpopular with his subjects who cared little that he rarely appeared in public towards the end of his reign.

William IV (1830-1837)

George's daughter and heir, Princess

LEFT: To raise the money to pay off his debts, George agreed to marry the wealthy Princess Caroline of Brunswick. When George saw her he was so appalled that he nearly fainted. After the birth of their only child, Princess Charlotte, the unhappy couple decided to separate.

1821–1822
The American Colonization Society founds the Liberian Republic in Africa for freed slaves.

1821–1832
The people of Greece, supported by Russia, France and Britain, gain freedom from the Ottoman Empire.

1822–1824
Simon Bolivar liberates Equador and Peru from Spanish rule. Bolivia is named after him.

Charlotte, died before her father. After his death the crown passed to his brother William, a very unlikely king. His many years in the navy had made him a rather gruff, unrefined man who tended to speak his mind, regardless of the consequences, which earned him the nickname 'The Sailor King'. But the people approved of William because he was like one of them.

Until his reign, only the richest and most powerful men and well-off farmers could vote in general elections. The new, prosperous, town-dwelling middle classes had been clamouring for the vote, but the Tories, backed by George IV, had refused to alter the law.

People hoped that the new king would

ABOVE: George IV spent his last years living quietly at his magnificent pavilion in Brighton or at Windsor Castle. Most days he did not rise until six in the evening, whereupon he got dressed, had supper – and went straight back to bed.

approve of the proposed reform, but he was as strongly opposed to it as his brother had been. Pressure became so strong that in 1832, with William's reluctant support, the Great Reform Act was passed by Parliament giving many more men the vote.

It was during his reign that slavery was abolished in the British colonies. William and his wife Adelaide had no children: when he died, his young niece Victoria came to the throne.

1829
Louis Braille, a French inventor and teacher of the blind, publishes his method of finger reading that enables blind people to 'read'.

1830
In France, the July Revolution removes Charles X from the throne. He is replaced by Louis Philippe, the Citizen King.

1830
The Belgians revolt against Dutch rule. Belgium becomes independent the following year.

VICTORIA

When Queen Victoria came to the throne in 1837, Britain was still a mainly rural country with small towns and villages linked by stage coaches. People travelled by horse and cart and most of them lived and worked in the countryside.

By the end of her long reign, cities such as Manchester and Sheffield had become so big that they spilled out into the countryside. The people who lived in them worked in factories. Railways criss-crossed the countryside, motor cars spluttered down the roads, gas lamps lit houses at night, and it was possible to speak to someone miles away on the telephone, and to travel underground across London.

As well as these obvious changes, there were other, less visible ones.

First, there was the power of the monarch. Unlike Elizabeth I, Queen Victoria had little real control. The country was ruled by Parliament and the cabinet, and although Parliament had to obtain her agreement to any laws they wanted to pass, the Queen could not tell the MPs and Lords what to do.

And then there was the power of the people. For centuries, agricultural workers had had very little say in what happened in their lives. But when they went to work in cities they began to realize that the factories and industries depended on their labour. They banded together into trade unions to demand better working conditions and pay. Some started their own businesses and became

LEFT: The coronation of Queen Victoria. After three elderly kings, the British were delighted to have someone young on the throne and packed the streets of London for the coronation procession.

1840
Under the Treaty of Waitangi, the Maori chiefs of New Zealand surrender the sovereignty of their country to the British government.

1842
Under the Treaty of Nanjing which ends the First Opium War, Chinese ports are opened to foreign trade and Britain gains control of Hong Kong.

1846
The Irish Potato Famine reaches its height. By 1851, more than one million Irish people will have died of starvation.

ABOVE: In 1851, Albert organized the Great Exhibition in London's Hyde Park.
The huge glass building that housed the displays of the latest machinery, technology and manufactured goods was known as the Crystal Palace.

prosperous. These people formed a thriving middle class and became an important influence in the way the country was run.

But back to Queen Victoria herself. The granddaughter of George III, she inherited the crown in 1837 at the age of eighteen.

In 1840 she fell in love with and married Prince Albert of Saxe-Coburg, and over the next 20 years they had nine children. In public, Albert came across as a rather stern and humourless man. In private, he was a strict father, but a loving husband.

He did a great deal for his adopted country and did much to turn Britain into a wealthy, manufacturing nation.

Victoria and Albert loved the countryside. They bought Osborne House on the Isle of Wight and Balmoral Castle in Scotland for their holidays, when they liked to pretend that they were just an ordinary family.

1848
The year of revolutions in Europe sees the people of France, Italy, Austria, Hungary and Poland rise against their governments.

1854
The Crimean War begins when Russia tries to gain control of part of the Ottoman Empire. Turkey, France and Britain join forces to prevent this.

1859
Charles Darwin publishes *On the Origin of Species* which introduces his controversial theory of natural selection.

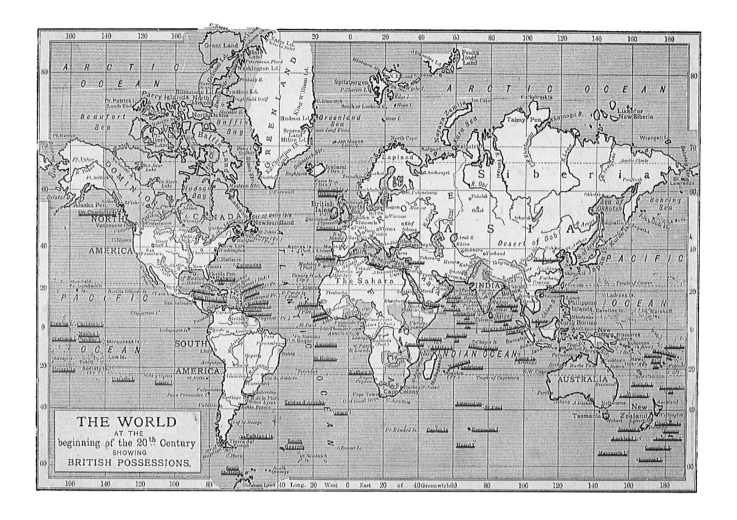

THE WORLD
AT THE
beginning of the 20th Century
SHOWING
BRITISH POSSESSIONS.

Both the Queen and her husband were conscientious workers. Victoria would not sign a document until she had read and understood it. She became expert in world affairs, often knowing more about them than the prime minister.

In 1861, Prince Albert died of typhoid. The Queen mourned his death so deeply that for years she refused to appear in public even for great state occasions. She was so upset that she insisted that his clothes were laid out every morning in his dressing room as they were during his life.

ABOVE: Queen Victoria was passionate about her Empire. It included India, parts of Africa, Australia, Canada and New Zealand. By 1900, all the parts coloured red on the map were British possessions.

At first everyone understood, but after a while their sympathy turned to irritation. Even *The Times* newspaper sided with the people when it published an article pointing out that the Queen owed it to her subjects to appear at such occasions as the State Opening of Parliament.

1859–1869
The Suez Canal is built by the French diplomat Ferdinand de Lesseps to link the Mediterranean with the Red Sea.

1861
Tsar Alexander II of Russia decrees that the serfs should be made free, and no longer bought and sold like slaves.

1861–65
The American Civil War begins when eleven southern states, determined to preserve slavery, break away from the rest of the United States.

40

While Victoria hid herself away, her son Edward, the Prince of Wales, became a more public figure. Like the previous Prince of Wales who had become George IV, he was a rather reckless young man. His behaviour had been such a constant concern to his father that Victoria blamed him for Albert's death.

There was such widespread disillusionment with the Royal Family that there was serious talk in many quarters that the monarchy should be abolished and Britain should become a republic. But before republican sympathies became deeply rooted, Victoria came out of her seclusion and returned to public life.

In 1887, her 50-year anniversary on the throne was joyfully celebrated in Britain and the Empire with extravagant festivities that demonstrated Britain's power to the world.

Ten years later, when she celebrated her Diamond Jubilee, rulers came from all over the world to congratulate her. Among the guests at the celebrations were almost a hundred of her own descendants. They included the Tsarina of Russia, the Kaiser of Germany and the Queens of Greece, Norway, Romania and Spain. It wasn't surprising that Victoria was known as the 'Grandmother of Europe'.

BELOW: Queen Victoria's funeral procession. When she died in 1901, after the longest reign of any British monarch, Britain had changed from being a rural society to a modern, industrial one. She was the first monarch to appear in a film, use a telephone, travel by train, use a lift, make a gramophone record, and have her photograph taken.

1864
The International Red Cross is founded in Switzerland to provide medical help for war victims.

1866
Alfred Nobel invents dynamite. He leaves the fortune he makes from it to be given as prizes for science, literature and peace.

1885
Karl Benz, the German inventor, builds the first petrol-driven motor-car. Most people want one, but only the very rich can afford them.

EDWARD VII & GEORGE V

Edward VII (1901-1910)

Edward VII was nearly 60 by the time Queen Victoria died and he came to the throne. He was a charming man, a great sportsman and a genial host.

Edward had little experience of government, but he was intelligent and sensible. Using his remarkable charm he convinced the French to agree an alliance with Britain, even though the countries had long been rivals. This earned him a reputation as a peacemaker.

He was the first British monarch to visit the United States.

He was far-sighted enough to see that the plans his ambitious nephew, the German Kaiser, had to make Germany the most powerful country in Europe, could lead to conflict. He did what he could to ensure that Britain was prepared for war.

Perhaps because his own childhood had been so unhappy, he was determined that his own children should be brought up in a happy, relaxed atmosphere. When he died, peacefully, in 1910, his son George mourned him as 'the best of friends and the best of fathers'.

George V (1910-1936)

When George's elder brother, Albert, died in 1892, George became heir to the throne.

George spent fifteen years in the navy, and by the time he came to the throne had probably seen more of the world than any other British monarch until then.

His reign was filled with dramatic events. In 1914, Europe was plunged into the First World War in which millions were killed.

Even before the war was over, in 1916, there was violent unrest in Ireland between those who wanted the country to remain part of the United Kingdom, and those who wanted independence. The result was that in 1922 the country was split into the two parts – the Irish Republic and Northern Ireland – that we know today.

1901
Australia is declared a Dominion. The new Australian Commonwealth becomes the first self-governing member of the British Empire.

1914
After the heir to the Austrian throne is assassinated, the First World War breaks out. By the time it ends millions of men and women will have been killed in action.

1917
The Russian Army turns against the Tsar, thus triggering the Russian Revolution which ends with the Communists led by Lenin in control.

By 1931, it was obvious the world was entering the deep economic recession known as the Depression. Millions of people lost their jobs. Businesses went bankrupt. Banks found themselves in desperate financial trouble.

The King did what he could to help. He brought the leaders of all the political parties together and urged them to find a solution to the problem. He toured the country to meet the people and see for himself what was going on.

Also, in 1931, it was decided that as ex-colonies such as Canada and Australia were now independent the name British Commonwealth should replace the former term British Empire.

In 1935, George V celebrated his Silver Jubilee – 25 years on the throne. He was genuinely surprised at the thousands of people who came on to the streets to cheer him. 'I'd no idea they felt like that about me. I'm beginning to think they like me for myself', he said.

The next year he died and his even more popular son, Edward VIII, took his place as king.

ABOVE: One of the most dramatic events of George V's reign occurred in 1917, when his Russian cousin Tsar Nicholas II was forced to abdicate. He and his family were held prisoner until 1918, when they were assassinated.

BELOW: George V was the first monarch to talk to his people on the radio on Christmas Day.

1919
After the horrors of the First World War, the League of Nations is formed to keep world peace.

1920
The production and consumption of alcohol are banned in the United States. Prohibition heralds the rise of gangsters such as Al Capone.

1933
The Nazi Party led by Adolf Hitler comes to power in Germany. Almost immediately, German Jews and gypsies are hounded and persecuted.

THE UNCROWNED KING & THE UNEXPECTED KING

Edward VIII (1936)

Edward VIII was a young man during the First World War. He pleaded with his father to let him fight in the trenches, but King George forbade it. But he was allowed to visit the front and saw some of the fighting. The bravery of the men and the suffering they were going through left a deep impression on him.

In the years after the war, he took an interest in the problems of some of the country's poorest people. During the Depression, his visits to stricken mining communities moved him. He had a real sympathy for his subjects, and many of them felt a tremendous loyalty to him.

In the mid-1930s he met and fell in love with an American woman, Wallis Simpson. Mrs Simpson had already been divorced once and later divorced her second husband.

Edward chose to give up the throne so that he could marry Mrs Simpson, which he did in France in 1937. He was granted the title Duke of Windsor, but the new duchess was never allowed to call herself Her Royal Highness, a snub which angered Edward for the rest of his life.

Apart from a short spell as Governor of the Bahamas during the Second World War, the Duke held no official positions. He and the Duchess made their home in France.

Edward only occasionally met his brothers and their families after he married Mrs Simpson. But when he died in 1972, his body was brought back to England and buried in the royal burial ground at Frogmore, alongside other kings. When the Duchess died, she was buried beside her husband.

George VI (1936-1952)

Albert, Duke of York, was not expected to become king, so he had had a freer life than his elder brother. As a young man he joined the navy and fought in the First World War,

---

BELOW: When Edward came to the throne he was determined to marry Mrs Simpson, but the prime minister, the Archbishop of Canterbury and other influential people knew that she would never be accepted as Queen. Edward chose to abdicate.

1936
Italian forces annex Ethiopia. The Emperor makes an emotional appeal for his country's freedom at the League of Nations.

 1939
After German troops invade Poland, Britain and France declare war on Germany. By the time the Second World War ends in 1945, 55 million people will have died.

 1945
The United Nations Organization is founded to maintain and promote international peace and security.

ABOVE: As often as possible, the King and the Queen visited families whose homes had been destroyed by German bombs. The Queen became especially popular. Her insistence on staying on in Britain and her trips to London's East End boosted morale so much that Hitler called her the most dangerous woman in Europe.

even though he suffered from seasickness. He later became a pilot in the air force, even though he did not really like flying!

He was a shy, serious man and he suffered from a nervous stutter. In 1923 he married Lady Elizabeth Bowes-Lyon and they had two daughters, Elizabeth and Margaret Rose. Lady Elizabeth, later known as the Queen Mother, became much loved by generations of British people.

The Duke and Duchess of York thoroughly enjoyed a happy family life which was destroyed when Edward abdicated and Albert came to the throne. He chose to be known as George VI.

He was daunted by the prospect of being king, but his wife was a constant encouragement and a pillar of strength, helping him to overcome his terrible stammer.

In 1939, Hitler's forces invaded Poland, an event that sparked off the Second World War. There were plans to evacuate the Queen and the two princesses to Canada. The Queen refused to listen to them, insisting that they all stayed in Britain.

The war ended in 1945. The Royal Family were no doubt looking forward to a long and happy reign, but sadly, the King's health began to fade. He was diagnosed as having lung cancer, and died in his sleep on 5th February 1952, after a day's shooting.

BELOW: By the time he died, George VI had become greatly loved by his subjects. Three queens mourned him at his funeral – his mother, Queen Mary; his wife, Queen Elizabeth; and his daughter, Queen Elizabeth II.

1947
India becomes independent of British rule when two new countries are created: the Hindu state of India and the Muslim state of Pakistan.

1948
The Jewish National Council proclaims the new state of Israel in the area known as Palestine. Almost immediately, Jews from all over the world go to live there.

1950–1953
The Korean War between North and South Korea is fought with the North backed by China and the South assisted by United Nations troops.

QUEEN ELIZABETH II

LEFT: Queen Elizabeth II and the Duke of Edinburgh, dressed in the robes of the Order of the Garter, ride in an open carriage at Windsor. The Order was founded by Edward III. Apart from members of the Royal Family, membership is restricted to 25 knights.

When the Duchess of York gave birth to a daughter in 1926, no one seriously thought that one day the little girl would become queen. But when her uncle, Edward VIII, abdicated and her father became king, she was heir to the throne.

She and her sister spent most of the war years at Windsor Castle. In 1945, Elizabeth joined the Auxiliary Transport Service where she learned car mechanics. She is without doubt the only British queen who could change the oil in a motor car if she had to!

After the war, the Princess fell in love with Prince Philip Mountbatten of Greece and they were married in 1947. The day before the wedding, Philip was created Duke of Edinburgh.

Early in 1952, the couple flew to Kenya on an official visit. They had been there only a few days when news came that Elizabeth's father had died.

When Elizabeth came to the throne, most Commonwealth countries were ruled directly by Britain. One of the first things she did on becoming queen was to tour these countries and meet her subjects there.

Today, all but a few Commonwealth countries have won their independence; Britain has no say in how they run their affairs, but the Queen, as head of the Commonwealth, retains a keen interest in them. In 1961 South Africa left the Commonwealth in the face of worldwide condemnation of its system of apartheid.

1953
Regular colour television broadcasts begin in the United States. Britain will have to wait another decade for colour television.

 1955
Black people in the southern United States begin to demand equality with white citizens. Eventually, Martin Luther King becomes their leader but is assassinated in 1968.

 1962
The USSR sets up nuclear weapons bases in Cuba. The Americans demand that they are dismantled and for a few days, until the Russians withdraw, the world hovers on the brink of nuclear war.

However, the new democratic Republic of South Africa, under the presidency of Nelson Mandela, rejoined the Commonwealth in 1994, and the Queen made a historic visit to South Africa in 1995 to celebrate this important event.

Although the Queen has no political power, she knows a lot about world affairs and politics, and has been known to give her prime ministers sound advice.

Unlike her father and grandfather, the Queen has not had to cope with any major wars during her reign. In the early years, there was a crisis over the control of the Suez Canal. British and French troops launched an unsuccessful invasion on Egypt. More recently, there has been the Falklands War, the Gulf War and the conflict in Bosnia.

At home, in 1968 the troubles in Ireland erupted with intense violence. In 1969 British troops were sent to the province in an attempt to contain the strife, but the bloodshed, and the conflict, continued. The 1998 Good Friday agreement promised peace and political progress, but it is yet to be seen if it will succeed.

The Queen has played an important part in attending remembrance events for the two World Wars. In 1995 she led many ceremonies to mark the fiftieth anniversary of the end of World War II.

The Royal Family has had its share of problems. Three of the Queen's children have divorced or separated, and the death of Diana, Princess of Wales, in a car accident in 1997 caused enormous grief across the country. The Princess's death was followed by much media discussion about the role of the monarchy in a changing society.

BELOW LEFT: Members of the Royal Family at the annual Trooping the Colour in June 1995.
BELOW RIGHT: The Prince and Princess of Wales with their two sons at a VJ Day parade to mark the 50th anniversary of the end of World War II.

1979
The Shah of Iran is forced into exile and an Islamic republic is established, headed by the Ayatollah Khomeini.

1990–91
Eastern European countries, including the USSR, free themselves from Communist control, and West Germany and East Germany unite after 45 years of separation.

1994
After 25 years of violence and killings in Northern Ireland, the IRA and Unionist terrorists declare a ceasefire.

INDEX

ACKNOWLEDGEMENTS

T=Top, B=Bottom, L=Left, R=Right, M=Middle
Bridgeman Art Library, 16, 23T, 24T, 29, 31L & R, 34;
J Allan Cash Photolibrary, 18;
East Sussex County Library, 37;
Mary Evans Picture Library, 5, 7T, 9, 10, 11, 15, 21, 26, 27B, 31M, 35, 41, 42;
Tim Graham 46;
Nunn Syndication 47;
Michael Holford, 7B;
Hulton Deutsch, 17, 27T, 40, 43, 44, 45;
Tony Stone Worldwide, 24B.

© 1991 HarperCollins*Publishers* Ltd
First published in 1991. Reprinted 1992, 1993, 1994, 1995, 1996, 1997, 1999 (twice), 2002, 2003, 2004

ISBN 000 198361 X

Printed and Bound by Printing Express Ltd., Hong Kong.

Cover portraits: (clockwise from top right) George IV, Elizabeth I: National Portrait Gallery; Elizabeth II: Bridgeman Art Library; Henry VIII, Charles I: National Portrait Gallery